WILL ROGERS

and the
Great White House Sleepover

Written by: Bart Taylor

Illustrated by: Greg White

Yorkshire Publishing
TULSA

ISBN: 978-1-954095-94-6 (Hardcover)
978-1954095-95-3 (Perfectbound)

Illustrated by: Greg White

For permission requests, write to the publisher at the address below.

Yorkshire Publishing

1425 E 41st Pl
Tulsa, OK 74105
www.YorkshirePublishing.com
918.394.2665

Published in the USA

This book would not have been possible without these folks:

Tad Jones
Jake Kruwiede
Jennifer Holt
Jennifer Rogers-Etcheverry
Andy Hogan
Will Rogers Memorial Museum Docents
Tim Taylor
Elizabeth Taylor
Lori Swindell
Scott Swindell
Tyler Palmateer
Ken Lane
Chris Segress
Kyle Krueger

Forward by Jennifer Rogers-Etcheverry

Great granddaughter of Will Rogers

I can recall learning about Will Rogers in my history books growing up in the small Midwest town of Tucumcari, New Mexico. Our family was very humble about the fact he was my great grandfather. To say that the words "Will Rogers" were rarely mentioned in our home is an understatement.

Fast forward to 1991 and the Broadway musical "Will Rogers Follies" opening night in New York City. My grandfather Jim, Will's youngest child, took our entire family all -thirteen of us- to "learn". It was that evening, sitting next to my grandfather, that I caught the W.R. bug and knew I had to learn more about this amazing man, my great grandfather.

As I became more and more involved in the Rogers family business my travels took me on frequent trips to the Will Rogers Memorial Museum in Claremore, Oklahoma. During one of these visits I was introduced to the museum's new intern, who was one of the youngest most energetic Will Rogers fans I have ever met, Bart Taylor. Bart's passion for Will is utterly infectious. Even if you have never heard of Will, after a few minutes with Bart you will be impressively educated and left wanting to learn more. Bart's personality along with his charm and wit has a likely connection to that of Will Rogers. Perhaps that's why this book is so fun to read. It tells the story of Will's visit and overnight stay in the White House. My first time reading "Will Rogers and the Great White House Sleepover" I felt the same excitement and energy as I did during that first meeting with Bart.

I hope that you experience the same excitement as you read and that you are left wanting to learn more about one of America's most favorite people.

Will Rogers is known to millions of people around the world for his colorful personality and many talents. He was a proud Cherokee who became famous as a stage and film actor, even performing on Broadway. But he was also a cowboy humorist, writer, social commentator, and early radio star who Oklahomans still know as their "Favorite Son."

Will also traveled the world. In 1926, he spent five months writing stories from Russia for the Saturday Evening Post, a popular magazine of the day where millions of Americans got their news. He arrived back in New York City on September 27th, 1926, and was in for a surprise.

Two days after returning from Russia, Will opened his mailbox and found an invitation from United States President Calvin Coolidge and the White House staff. The note read, "The President hopes you will stay at the White House."

Will couldn't believe it! He was nervous and excited at the same time. He joked, "Just think, I'll be the only non-office seeker that ever slept in the White House!" Invitations to the White House were usually reserved for official ambassadors — not cowboys from Oklahoma.

Would he and the President have anything in common? Will knew the President was known for being a bit stiff and quiet, but Will always said he never met a man he didn't like!

So, Will set off on his GREAT adventure to stay the night at the White House. He still couldn't believe he and the President were going to sit down, talk and get to know each other.

Will's train ride to Washington D.C. was running a bit late, but he didn't mind. He couldn't stop smiling through the window at all the famous landmarks.

What famous landmarks do you know of in Washington D.C.? Can you name the ones in the picture?

Will Rogers was raised in a large white house called the "White House on the Verdigris."

So when it came time to visit the REAL White House, he thought he could walk in the front door just like he was at home!

What would you bring with you on a sleepover to the White House? Do you think it would be hard to sleep?

As Will walked in the front door he heard dogs barking, birds chirping and little paws scurrying and bounding down the stairs.

The President had numerous pets such as dogs, cats, raccoons and birds. Because he grew up on a ranch, Will began to feel right at home.

The President was nicknamed "Silent Cal" because of his reserved personality. When Will noticed the President quietly waiting to welcome him to the White House, Will exclaimed, "Hi, Cal!" The President seemed nervous at first but he quickly realized there was no reason to worry.

The President knew the power of Will's writings and understood that Will, like nobody else, could show the country his true character. The President wanted people to know he was a normal human being just like them.

For dinner, Will and the President walked to the dining hall where they would share a fish dinner.

Will noticed that the President loved his dogs and kept feeding them table scraps throughout the meal.

Seeing this, Will started to laugh! He couldn't help but feel right at home watching the President relax around his dogs.

After all, Will always said, "I love a dog, he does nothing for political reasons!"

After their fish dinner, the President and Will retired to the President's study to unwind and relax.

Will knew what an honor it was to be invited to spend time alone with the President, so Will wanted to impress him with rope tricks and a few "yarns," which Will called his jokes.

Will and the President didn't agree on politics and had different personalities, but it didn't matter. They found common ground through humor, storytelling and animals.

They talked for hours into the early morning, and laughed until they both cried. Will shared stories of his recent time in Russia and the President told a few of his favorites. It was turning into a night Will Rogers would never forget!

When President Coolidge went to bed, Will stayed wide awake. He wanted to explore the White House more, so he decided to tour it all by himself.

Will couldn't believe his eyes when he walked into the Oval Office. IT WAS GREEN! Ever since 27th U.S. President William Howard Taft had taken office, the Oval Office had an all green interior.

Will loved to learn about American history. In fact, as a child at Kemper Military School, he made a perfect grade in his history class. He stood in awe at the Oval Office and wondered how many important moments in U.S. history had happened here.

Will slept in the White House's large guest room, which had a bathroom, and a dressing room with a small bed in it. Will didn't want to mess up the larger bed, so he slept in the smaller bed in the dressing room.

Tucked in bed, Will kept thinking about his favorite U.S. President, Abraham Lincoln. To help himself sleep, he counted "Lincolns" instead of sheep!

Did you know Will was a friend to many different U.S. Presidents? How many Presidents can you name?

24

Will would write several articles for the Saturday Evening Post about his experience at the White House. The articles gave Americans their first glimpse inside the White House and a behind-the-scenes look at the life of a sitting President.

In his writings, Will reassured Americans that President Coolidge was like them and not some "European King living in splendor!"

Will Rogers would become friends with many different Presidents throughout the course of his life.

Presidents Wilson, Harding, Coolidge, Hoover and Franklin Roosevelt all recognized Will's ability to sway public opinion with his words.

Will wrote about politics through humor, and convinced Americans that this wasn't just entertainment, it was in fact an essential service for strengthening democracy.

Will loved his country and always said, "America is the land of opportunity and don't ever forget it!" What words could you use to describe your love for our country?

Printed in the USA
CPSIA information can be obtained
at www.ICGtesting.com
LVHW061051121123

763674LV00025B/101